ABHINANDAN PATIL

Software Engineering for Communication Network Engineers

First edition

This book was professionally typeset on Reedsy.
Find out more at reedsy.com

Contents

Dedication

To my Family members, Well Wishers and Teachers in that Order.

Acknowledgement

Author Acknowledges his past organizations for giving opportunity to explore the world of Wireless communication. The Author acknowledges the Books referenced in this work. Author Acknowledges his colleagues in Phoenix, Arizona and Chicago, Illinois for their initial help in understanding the Java Network Simulator.

Author also acknowledges Reedsy for providing great software for typesetting the content. Author acknowledges Kubuntu Operating System, Libre Draw and Mozilla browsers.

Preface

Author of this Book has vast experience in emulators for Wireless Networks. Software Engineering is interesting subject but the treatment of the subject is bit skewed towards web development and web testing as is evident from many software engineering books and papers. Therefore the Author tries to shed light on the subject from communication network engineering perspective. Where possible Author mentions how the software engineering was practiced in his organizations. This Book is basically for advanced professionals with the knowledge of Software Engineering, Communication Networks, Foundations of Software Testing, Network Programming and some one with brief knowledge of Satellite Communication. Author explains how his work in Wireless Network Organization could be used for forward looking projects like satellite communication systems testing etc along with terrestrial networks for communication testing. Introduction chapter is dedicated to what the projects were in his past organization so that readers are on the same page as Author when he discusses the principle and practices of software engineering. So it the Book is partly past and partly forward looking towards the satellite communication. This Book does NOT contain proprietary information of Authors past organization so Author does NOT violate any of his past agreements with his past organizations. No Organization's internal consumption only matter is discussed in the Book. I am sure this book will be of benefit to Authors Readers.

About Author

Dr. Abhinandan H. Patil is Founder and CTO of Technology Firm in India, Karnataka. Before this, he has worked in Wireless Network Software Organization as Lead Software Engineer for close to a decade. His Research out put is available as Books and Thesis in IJSER, USA. He is Active Researcher in the field of Machine Learning, Deep Learning, Data Science, Artificial Intelligence, Regression Testing applied to Networks, Communication and Internet of Things. He is active contributor of Science, Technology, Engineering and Mathematics. He is currently working on few Undisclosed Books. In the capacity as CTO of organization He carries out Research activity. He has started Blogging recently on Technology and Allied Areas. He is nominated for RULA Research Award. He is Adarsh Vidya Saraswati Rashtriya Puraskar Awardee in year 2020. Dr. Abhinandan H. Patil is Senior IEEE member since 2013 and is member of Smart Tribe and Cheeky Scientists Association. Dr. Patil has had two long stints in USA supporting commercial releases of Mobility Manager where he was Single Point of Contact for Java Network Simulator.

Dr. Abhinandan H. Patil can be visited at https://abhinandanhpatil.info and his personal email ID is Abhinandan_patil_1414@yahoo.com

1

Introduction

F ew Books before we can even start:

1. Software Engineering by Roger S. Pressman
2. Mobile Network Engineering GSM, 3G-WCDMA, LTE and The Road to 5G by Alexander KukuShin
3. Foundations of Software Testing by Rex Black
4. Software Architecture for Developers by Simon Brown
5. Computer Networks by Andrew S. Tanenbaum
6. Satellite Communication Systems Engineering by Louis J. Ippolito Jr.
7. Unix Network Programming by W. Richard Stevens

I will be discussing Software Engineering "for" Communication Network Engineers. I will be discussing about two of my Industrial Projects done during 2001-2009 time frame and I will be explaining how they are still relevant and in particular how the network simulator could be communication network generation agnostic.

1.1 Project for UMTS UE

To begin consider the following Universal Mobile Terrestrial Signalling Architecture.

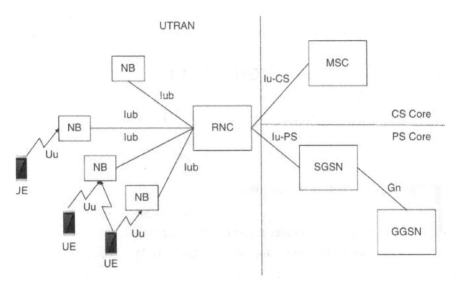

UMTS Architecture

Clearly it has Access and Non Access Stratum. So to test the Universal Terrestrial Radio Access Network we need either actual User Equipment or its Emulator. This emulator will run on the Board with VxWorks Operating System. VxWorks also provided VxSim which was simulator of the VxWorks Operating System which could be run on actual Unix System. Our work for Network service provider in Spain involved development of UE Simulator ahead of actual UE availability date so that Network team could test the UTRAN. I worked for process called command line interface which would be used to trigger the UESim. Also I developed code for the Mobile Protocol Manager, third layer of UE. CLI work involved constructing the byte stream as per the Interface Control Document or ICD in short to be communicated with MPM.

The MPM work involved Quality of Service measurement etc as per the UMTS Specification.

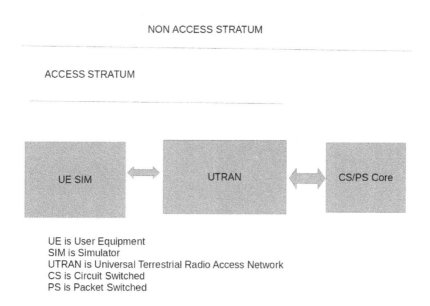

NON ACCESS STRATUM

ACCESS STRATUM

UE SIM ⟺ UTRAN ⟺ CS/PS Core

UE is User Equipment
SIM is Simulator
UTRAN is Universal Terrestrial Radio Access Network
CS is Circuit Switched
PS is Packet Switched

UMTS UESimulator

1.2 JAVA Network Simulator Project

This project was for testing the Mobility Manager or MM in short of Code Division Multiple Access Network. MM is heart of CDMA network and deemed to be the most complex Box of CDMA network. I am giving architecture of Java Network Simulator below. This was for Motorola Network of CDMA 3G1x.

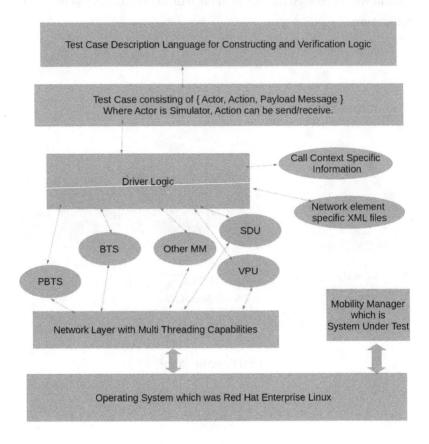

JAVA Network Simulator

The simulator mentioned above could be used for the following Evolved Packet System by incorporating the appropriate changes. 3G was Circuit + Packet. 4G is all IP. So addition simulator modules will be required to test the Evolved Packet System. No need to remove the legacy simulators. They will be useful for testing backward compatibility.

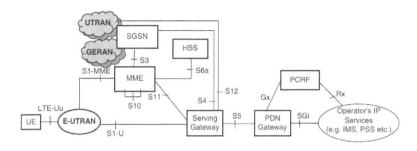

Evolved Packet System in Long Term Evolution

If we look at the stack of TCP/IP, following layers will be evident. The Link layer could be 3g, 4g, 5g or even satellite in our test setup. To accommodate satellite communication capability in host based system additional Radio capable board will be required. Or whole Java Network Simulator can be on embedded board with adequate capability.

APPLICATION LAYER IN OUR CASE SIMULATOR TOOL
TRANSPORT LAYER TCP or UDP
INTERNET LAYER IP/ICMP
LINK LAYER COULD BE ETHERNET, WiMAX, 3G/LTE/5G or SATELLITE COMMUNICATION

TCP/IP Model Link Layer Could be WiMAX, LTE, 5G or even Satellite Communication

Summary: We need special hardware board which will have capability to send and receive network packets to and from Satellite Network. Therefore the Java Network Simulator is generation agnostic with appropriate enhancements. With that understanding let us see how Software Engineering subject fares with respect to the above mentioned two projects which I will be taking as case studies.

2

Authors List of Partial Past Projects

Some of the projects that I can recollect which are relevant to this Book are as follows

- Custom parsers for Variable Call Detail Log
- Release migration Shell scripts which brought down process from 20 days to 1 day
- Reduced configuration file entries
- Implemented Automation where frame work would bring up tool, execute the test cases, collected call detail logs and name them appropriately, collected resource manager logs and name them appropriately etc. Raised alarm through mail in the event of failures, send the group mail after completion of Automation etc
- Built solid Rapo with customer. Enhanced the image of Indian Team in the eyes of the customer etc.
- Attempted and succeeded in converting functionality testing tool to load testing tool
- Implemented Mobile Assisted Hand Off with zero defects.
- Removed the additional tool expect and implemented the logic in network simulator itself.
- Meaningless Enhancement Request were turned down with valid data.

Few other notable things were:

- Project lead had given estimation of 4 months with 5 resources for fixing
- the Logging bug. Which I fixed with single line by fixing the lower layer
- Team had given bloated estimation for mutation testing. I showed the way to do that using network layer.
- The above mentioned bullet helped in sending two successive messages with less than nano seconds delay
- Defended the team where required. We had test manager who used to say large number of scripts would be impacted for any improvement in simulator tool etc. At one point I wrote shell script which scanned all the test cases and showed that the number of test cases impacted because of the proposed enhancement was two. Yes you read it correct. only 2/2000 test cases were impacted.

Summary: Author discusses about his partial list of projects and his suitability to write this Book.

3

What is Software and Software Engineering

People with hardware background can understand software better. People with hardware background would have encountered hard wired logic. By putting different firmware in micro controller for example you can make the same hardware behave differently. In general software brings flexibility to hardware. The other way of looking at it is software powers hardware. Can you imagine your workstation or laptop without Operating System? That is software is essential for hardware and vice versa.

Engineering in general involves systematic, disciplined and quantifiable approach towards problem solution. Software Engineering is marriage of Software and Engineering.

Software can be for specific purpose:

- System software
- Application software
- Engineering and Scientific software
- Web application
- Artificial Intelligence Software
- Communication Software

Software Process Involves following:

- Inception phase: Begins with project kick off and involves requirements gathering
- Planning: Involves work schedule, Artifacts to be produced list, planning for resources required and listing likely risks.
- Modeling: Architecture and/or design.
- Execution: Actual implementation. Example Manual coding or code generation
- Deployment: Delivery to customers

According to David Hooker, roughly software engineering practice is summarized by following principles.

- Think the reason for existence of software
- Keep It Simple Stupid
- Vision
- Software is for others to consume
- Forward vision towards future
- Plan ahead for Reuse
- Think

You can add to David's list as necessary to cater your organization's needs.

Summary: We discussed what is software and software engineering. Software Process, Software Engineering Practice and Software category. We are interested in software category meant for communication networks.

4

Software Process Models

S alient software processes in practice today are:

1. Waterfall model: Progress trickles like water right from Inception, planning, architecture/design, implementation(including testing) and deployment
2. V model: Here Acceptance test cases are designed at the same time as Requirements.System test cases are written at the same as product high level design. Integration test cases are written at the same time as low level design. Unit test cases are written at the same time as coding by developers.
3. Incremental Process: Software Process is incremental in nature.
4. Evolutionary such as prototyping, spiral model
5. Concurrent model: Here the individual steps of software engineering are parallelized to maximum extent possible.
6. Combination of 1. through 5

V model is most suited for communication software. 2 can be combined to some extent with 3,4 or 5 but base model is V model as I will explain. For example we had Global Software Group and individual locations were meant for developing one Box of the whole system. What I mean by Box? It could be Mobility Manager or Packet Base Transceiver Station. So {Phoenix,Chicago and India} developed MM while Poland was responsible for Packet Base Transceiver Station. That way it is concurrent model. However process within a given Box was always V model. Hope this is making sense. At the inception of the project it could be prototyping to deliver the prototype but final delivery is still V.

Till now we have viewed the process model for a given geographical location. These are team software process while individual engineer could be following different process.

Given process leads to final product.

Summary: V model in combination with other process model was followed in my communication network software organization.

5

Agile Development Practices

gile manifesto.org lists the Agile principles

1. Our highest priority is to satisfy the customer through early and continuous delivery of valuable software. // Comments: For communication software there is no continuous deliver

2. Welcome changing requirements, even late in development. Agile processes harness change for the customer's competitive advantage.// Comments: Changed requirements in Communication software is failure on part of requirement gathering. There could be few exceptions but it cannot be norm

3. Deliver working software frequently, from a couple of weeks to a couple of months, with a preference to the shorter timescale.//-Comments: There are no frequent deliveries in communication software

4. Business people and developers must work together daily throughout the project.//Comment: This holds good.

5. Build projects around motivated individuals.Give them the environment and support they need, and trust them to get the job done.//Comment: This is fine

6. The most efficient and effective method of conveying infor-

mation to and within a development team is face-to-face conversation.//Comment: May not be true for geographically spread development teams. If zoom/MSTeam/Google meet are face to face fine

7. Working software is the primary measure of progress.

8. Agile processes promote sustainable development. The sponsors, developers, and users should be able to maintain a constant pace indefinitely.//Comment: Not true for communication software

9. Continuous attention to technical excellence and good design enhances agility.

10. Simplicity—the art of maximizing the amount of work not done—is essential.

11. The best architectures, requirements, and designs emerge from self-organizing teams.

12. At regular intervals, the team reflects on how to become more effective, then tunes and adjusts its behavior accordingly.

So few Agile principles are fine for communication software all the principals cannot be employed as they are.

Summary: While Agile has its own takers in other category of software primarily application software, it has many draw backs for communication software.

6

Understanding Requirements

D esigning and building software in general is challenging, creative. The broad spectrum of tasks and techniques that lead to understanding of requirements is requirement engineering.

Requirements Engineering consists of:

1. Inception: During this phase stake holders define business case for the idea, try to identify breadth and depth of the market, do feasibility study and identify project scope

2. Elicitation: Ask customer what the objective for system are, what to be accomplished, how the system fits the need of the business finally how the system needs to be used on day to day basis

3. Elaboration: The information obtained during Inception and Elicitation is expanded and refined.

4. Specification: Specification can be written document, graphical model, mathematical model, uses cases a prototype or any combination of these.

5. Validation: Product is validated in this step.

Summary: This chapter discusses about understanding requirements

7

Requirements Modeling

Basically General Software Engineering Books classify the requirement modeling into following types.

1. Scenario based: Requirement modeling based on various scenarios.

2. Data Models: Basically concentrates on information domain for the problem

3. Class oriented: Object Oriented Classes. How Classes interact etc. This may not be true as communication software are implemented using C etc

4. Flow oriented: Basically Data Flow. In communication we are interested in message exchanges

5. Behavioral: How system behaves to external events. This is fine as communication software are generally Finite State Machine (FSM) based.

Summary: Not all communication software requirements are gathered using Unified Modeling Language.

8

System Architecture

System Architecture has slightly different meaning in communication software:

System Architecture generally involves breaking the given system into boxes. This is in adherence of standards such as partnership projects. Basic aim is inter operability between vendors. Example: Seamless hand over from service provider to service provider etc. There are minimum requirements to be met over and above which networking software vendor can give additional features etc. There are constraints to be met.

Summary: This chapter is about System Architecture. Software Architecture is next chapter.

9

Software Architecture

Within a given box what mechanism should be used for Inter Process Communication

- Pipes
- Message Queues
- Shared Memory
- Sockets
- Semaphores etc.

How many Processes the Box should have?

What Operating System should be used for given Box? What programming language for required

- Throughput
- Availabilty
- Scalability
- Performance
- Security
- Maintainability
- Power consumption and power dissipation

These are all Architectural Decisions.

Summary: We discussed about software architecture.

10

Design

After Architecture comes design and involves:

1. Abstraction
2. Patterns only if applicable
3. Separation
4. Modularity
5. Refinement
6. Refactoring
7. cohesion
8. Coupling

PLEASE BEWARE Unified Modeling Language (UML in short) is not must for communication software.

Also, Design must take care of:

1. Usability: Software should be usable
2. Functionality: It should function as intended
3. Reliability: Software should be reliable. Remember six 9s
4. Efficiency: Software should be efficient
5. Maintainability: Software should be maintainable to handle attrition etc

in Organization

Summary: This chapter discusses about Software design.

11

Quality Concepts

Software Quality, rather difficult term to define is an intangible attribute of software which decides the success or failure of the product/organization in general is mainly decided by the effectiveness of software testing and process followed in the project or organization. Software Quality revolution started in Japan/USA simultaneously. The earliest documents date back to as early as 1950.

According to McCall Quality Factors Involve:

1. Correctness
2. Reliability
3. Efficiency
4. Integrity
5. Usability
6. Maintainability
7. Flexibility
8. Portability
9. Reusability
10. Interoperability

All the 10 factors are relevant for relevant for communication software. And these 10 factors are intuitive.

Software Quality Dilemma involve

1. Good Enough Software: Software Testing will never be complete. So many organizations "some" time release software with release note mentioning the limitations and workarounds etc
2. The cost of Quality: Two types of costs are involved time and money. Cost of Quality should be taken into account
3. Risks. According to Roger Pressman " People bet their jobs, their comforts, their safety, their entertainment, their decisions and their very lives on computer software". SO TRUE
4. Quality and Security:As system grows complex Quality and Security are foremost important
5. Management Decisions: These include the following which must be correct

- Estimation decisions
- Scheduling decisions
- Risk Oriented decisions

Achieving Software Quality

The following are required for achieving required software quality for communication software.

1. Software Engineering Methods
2. Project Management Techniques
3. Quality Control
4. Quality Assurance

Summary: We started with definition of Quality. We listed McCalls Quality Factors. We discussed Software Quality dilemma. We also discussed what should be done to achieve software quality.

12

Review Techniques

T he sole purpose of review techniques is to reduce software defects.

- Fixing defects involves cost
- Defects amplify as they percolate to next stage in the software process

Like any activity in software engineering, review effectiveness can be quantified using review metrics. Many review metrics can be derived with the help of:

- Preparation effort
- Assessment effort
- Rework effort
- Work product size
- Minor defects
- Major defects

For example for code review these include time spent by the review team preparing and assessing. Rework time taken by the Author of the code. Work product size quantified using Kilo Lines of Code. Minor/Major defects found during the review and fixed later by the Author.

Reviews can be formal or informal.

Summary: This chapter discusses about Review Techniques.

13

Software Quality Assurance

S oftware Quality Assurance encompasses range of activities such as:

1. Standards: IEEE/ISO
2. Reviews and audits with the intent of uncovering errors
3. Software testing with primary goal of finding bugs.
4. Defect collection and analysis with the intention how to avoid defects
5. Education of stake holders for better quality
6. Vendor management to tailor the external software for specific needs of organization
7. Security management to protect the privacy of end customers
8. Risk management to mitigate the risks.

SQA Goals and Metrics

1. Requirement quality : Correctness, completeness and consistency
2. Design Quality: Is adequate, correct and meets the requirements
3. Code quality: Must confirm to coding standards and should be maintainable
4. Quality control: Is effective

Statistical Software Quality Assurance

Notable is Six Sigma and was pioneered by my organization. Which is defined as " A rigorous and disciplined methodolgy that uses data and statistical analysis to measure and improve company's operation performance by identifying and eliminating defects".

Software Reliability measures for Communication Software

This is mean time between failure MTBF and MTBF is MTTF + MTTR where MTTF is Mean Time To Failure and MTTR is Mean Time To Recovery.

Thus Availability is $[(MTTF)/(MTTF+MTTR)] \times 100 \%$

Summary: We discussed Software Quality Assurance, SQA Goals and metrics, Statistical SQA and Software Reliability measure for Communication software.

14

Software Testing Strategies

I n this chapter I will be discussing few NON communication software testing strategies which can be applied to communication network software as well

Why Software Quality Assurance aka Software Testing is third chapter in this Book? Soon you will know. But for the time being Software Testing is as essential as development.

One thing that has not changed in the last 25 years is the fact that software testing is lion share of total budget of software life cycle. If we have to quantify it, its is 50+%. In academic circles, software testing was small chapter in software engineering books. Today you see books and dedicated post graduate courses being offered in software testing. A look at the number of books in Reference section or search on search engines for postgraduate courses should justify this fact.

In this chapter we shall touch upon theory and practices that lead to production grade software. We shall also talk about requirements, defects, test cases, test results, verification of software against requirements and validation of software against test oracles etc. Then we shall move on to Unit, Integration, System and Acceptance testing.

Software Quality, rather difficult term to define is an intangible attribute of software which decides the success or failure of the product/organisation in general is mainly decided by the effectiveness of software testing and process followed in the project or organisation. Software Quality revolution started in Japan/USA simultaneously. The earliest documents date back to as early as 1950. The earliest documents are Shewart's cycle which talks about PDCA (Short for Plan, Do, Check and Act) and Ishikawa diagram which is essentially { {Materials, Methods}, {Machines, Measurements}} -> Quality. Where { } means combined and -> means leads to.

Software testing can be

- Static as in code inspection and code review
- Dynamic as in Actual execution to expose failure

The other thing that is talked much about is Fault -> Error -> Failure or Fault leads to Failure in short. Example developer trying to divide number by 0 or trying to access the memory out of bounds in C programming language are Faults and the resulting core dump is example of Failure.

Another important attribute of software is reliability. We often hear about telecom networking companies talking about 99.9999% up time which is essentially reliability of the software. The main objective of the testing is to catch the bugs and catch them early, to reduce risk and reduce cost of testing.

What is Test Case?

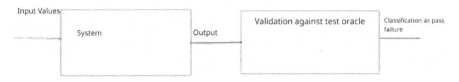

Test Case Illustrated

As shown in the diagram above, test case consists of input values or test data and system accepts this input and produces output which then is validated against the test oracle to classify the execution of test case as pass or failure.

Two popular software models are V and Agile. We shall take up Agile later. Let us take a look at V model and see which testing phase fits where.

V Model:

- Acceptance test cases are designed at the same time as Requirements.
- System test cases are written at the same as product high level design
- Integration test cases are written at the same time as low level design
- Unit test cases are written at the same time as coding by developers

Yet another term we often hear about testing is Regression testing. Regression testing is the activity which is carried out to ensure that any new functionality introduced does not break existing code or existing functionality. Or in other words with new functionality system should not regress. Regression testing can be at Unit, Integration or System testing level.

Next is how do we design the test cases?. Test cases are ideally designed on the basis of requirement specifications. Other sources could be code (White box approach) or the basis of input-output domain(Black box). Planning, Design, Monitoring and Measurement are the important phases of testing.

What are test tools? Anything and everything that leads to increased test productivity of tester, leads to better coverage, results in reduction of duration test phases, leads to increased effectiveness can be classified as test Tool.

Now let us touch upon some of the industry specific certifications:

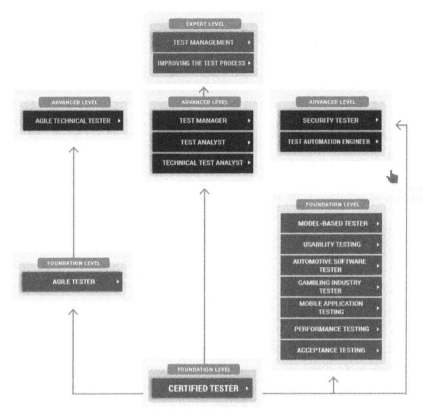

ISTQB Certification Portfolio

In this book we will be covering core track:

- Certified Tester Foundation Level
- Test Analyst
- Test Manager

We will be touching upon Agile track with:

- Agile Tester Foundations

3.1 Certified Tester Foundation Level

The certification tests testers on three parameters

- K1: Remeber
- K2: Understand
- K3: Apply

Syllabus for the same is

- Chapter 1: 175 minutes Fundamentals of Testing
- Chapter 2: 100 minutes Testing Throughout the Software Development Lifecycle
- Chapter 3: 135 minutes Static Testing
- Chapter 4: 330 minutes Test Techniques
- Chapter 5: 225 minutes Test Management
- Chapter 6: 40 minutes Tool Support for Testing

Now let us see what they cover.

3.1.1 Fundamentals of Testing

- Necessity of testing: Humans and others are causes of software defects. Human actions result in error. Error leads to Defect or bug. Defect leads to failure. This is already mentioned.
- Role of testing on product quality: The effective testing and product quality are related.
- Exhaustive testing will never be a possibility. Testing has to be concluded at some logical point
- Testing consists of following activities:

1. Test planning: This is the activity during which scope, approach, resources and schedule are established.

2. Test control: Any deviation from test plan is corrected in this activity
3. Test Analysis: Identify what to test
4. Test Design: Activity to determine how to test what is decided to be tested. Activity where test plan is translated into tangible test cases
5. Test implementation: Developing and prioritising test procedures, test data and setting up test environment.
6. Test execution: Actual test execution.
7. Checking results: Checking results and outcome of test execution
8. Evaluating the exit criteria: Where quality needs are balanced against other project priorities and constraints.
9. Test results reporting: Reporting test progress against exit criteria
10. Test closure: This is when closure is done with relevant test metrics and re-usable test wares etc.

- Seven Testing principles

1. Principle 1: Testing process shows the presence of defects and it cannot prove the absence of defects.
2. Principle 2: Exhaustive testing is impossible.
3. Principle 3: Start the testing early
4. Principle 4: Defects tend to be clustered
5. Principle 5: Pesticide paradox: Same testing repeated over and again will no longer find the new defects.
6. Principle 6: Testing is context sensitive meaning testing for health care and safety critical testing will not be the same
7. Principle 7: Absence of errors fallacy: If the software is error free but unusable and if it does not meet users expectations it is zero sum.

Attributes of tester and Code of Ethics. Following are the traits of testers

1. Curiosity
2. Critical eye
3. Detail oriented

4. Experience
5. Good communication

In addition to these testers must possess highest level of ethics.

3.1.2 Testing throughout the software life cycle

According to the accepted prevailing knowledge, testing at the end of life cycle as in case of water fall model is inadequate. There fore the models that employ testing throughout the life cycle are employed. One such model is V model which is already discussed.

Test levels:

1. Component testing. Also called Unit testing or module testing Makes use of stub and drivers. Stub is called component and driver is calling component.
2. Integration testing. Testing designed to expose defects in component interaction or component interfaces.
3. System testing. Behaviour of the whole system or product is tested.
4. Acceptance testing. It is a formal testing with respect to user needs and requirements.

Testing types:

1. Functional testing: Cross checking the functionality of component or system against specifications
2. Non functional testing: Testing reliability, usability, efficiency, main-tainability, security and portability
3. Structural testing: Measuring the thoroughness with respect to coverage items. Code coverage is an example of structural testing with respect to code.

4. Conformation testing and Regression testing

3.1.3 Static testing techniques:

Static testing is a testing where component or system is tested without execution. It is opposite of dynamic testing where actual execution of component or system is done.

- Review process:

1. Review process consists of Planning, kick-off, preparation, review meeting, rework and follow-up.
2. Moderator, Author, reviewer and manager are roles of review process
3. Walk through and inspection are types of review

- Static Analysis by Tools

1. Process of checking the code for adherence to coding standards
2. Checking code metrics with respect to cyclomatic complexity etc.
3. Checking control flow structure, data flow structure and data structures etc.

3.1.4 Test design techniques

In Test design we encounter important term called test case specification where test cases are specified with respect to objective, inputs, expected results and execution preconditions. Another important term is traceability which maps the items in documents to software item.

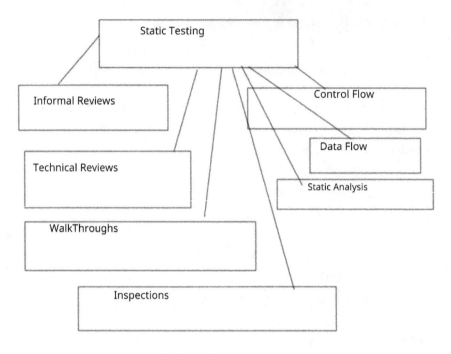

Static testing techniques

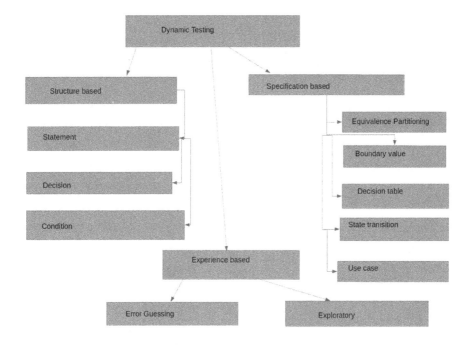

Dynamic Testing Techniques

Test development process would consist of

- Test Analysis where test conditions are analysed
- Test design
- Test implementation

Following are categories of test design tecchniques

- Static testing: Where no test cases are executed and generally done before test cases are executed on software
- Specification based, black box
- Structure based, white box
- Experience based

Now let us look at each one of them in detail.

Specification based or black box testing techniques

· Equivalence partitioning and boundary value analysis:

In this approach input or output domain are divided into partitions and test cases are designed to represent the each of these partitions. If this definition is difficult to understand, let us take a concrete example. Let us take banks interest rate as an example. Let us say bank pays 3% interest rate for deposit up to $100, 5% for deposit greater than $100 but less than $1000, 7% for deposit in excess of $1000. We have to design test cases for each of these cases. We may also want to test for $99.9, $100.1, $999.9, $1000.1. These are boundary values and testing technique is named accordingly as boundary value analysis

New customer (15%)	Loyalty card (10%)	Coupon (20%)	Discount(%)
T	T	T	Not possible
T	T	F	Not possible
T	F	F	20%
T	F	T	15%
F	T	T	30%
F	T	F	10%
F	F	T	20%
F	F	F	0

Decision table based testing

Let us take credit card with following discount policy

1. New customer gets 15% discount
2. Existing customer with loyalty card gets 10% discount
3. If the customer has coupon 20% discount

Discount amounts are added if applicable

Decision Table for Credit Card Example

Now test cases need to be added for each of the cases of Decision table

.

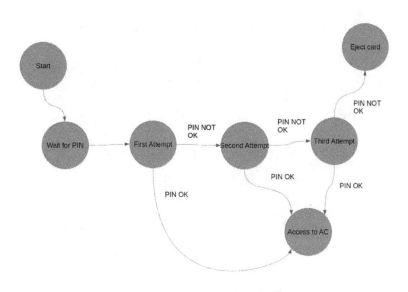

State transition diagram based testing

State transition for PIN entry

State transition testing is black box approach where valid and invalid state transitions are tested with unique test cases. State transition diagram shows the various states of component or system and events that cause the state transition. Telecom system software comprises some of the most complex state transition diagrams.

- Use case based testing

Use case based testing is a black box approach where test cases are designed to execute scenarios of use cases.

- Structure or white box based testing

Is as mentioned in the head lines is white box based testing approach. It is coverage based where coverage is defined as follows:

Coverage = Number of coverage items exercised/Total number of coverage items

1. Statement coverage: Statement coverage= Number of statements exercised/Total number of statements.
2. Decision coverage: Decision coverage= Number of decision outcomes exercised/Total number of Decisions.
3. Branch coverage: Branch coverage= Number of branches exercised/Total number of Branches

- Experience based testing technique

1. Error guessing
2. Exploratory testing : An informal approach where tester uses the information and knowledge gained while testing to further improve the test design and test cases

- Choosing test technique

There is test technique which fits all the needs all the time. Each test technique has its own advantages and benefits. Combination of test techniques can be used depending upon the need of testing.

3.1.5 Test management

Test management involves planning, estimating, monitoring and control of test activities. Test Manager(Test Leader) is the one who is at the helm of these activities. Let us look at the each components one by one.

· Test Planning

This is the first step of test management. Let us look at how the test plan document looks like:

Test Plan according to IEEE 829-1998

1. Test plan identifier
2. Introduction
3. Test items
4. Features to be tested
5. Features not to be tested
6. Approach
7. Item pass/fail criteria (test exit criteria)
8. Suspension criteria and resumption requirements
9. Test deliverables
10. Testing tasks
11. Environmental needs
12. Responsibilities
13. Staffing and training needs
14. Schedule
15. Risk and contingencies
16. Approvals

IEEE 829 Test Plan Template

The IEEE 829-1998 template is self explanatory and explains test plan documents outline.

- Test Estimation

This process is estimating what testing will involve and how much it will cost.

- Test Monitoring and Control

This activity involves monitoring and control. Test logs and test reports aid this activity

IEEE 829 STANDARD: TEST LOG TEMPLATE

Test log identifier	Activity and event entries (execution
Description (items being tested,	description, procedure results
environment in which the testing is	environmental information
conducted)	anomalous events, incident report
	identifiers)

IEEE 829 Test Log Template

IEEE 829 STANDARD:
TEST SUMMARY REPORT TEMPLATE

Test summary report identifier	Evaluation
Summary	Summary of activities
Variances	Approvals
Comprehensive assessment	
Summary of results	

IEEE 829 Test Summary Report

Yet another term that we encounter is incident management.

Incident management is the process of recognising, investigating, taking actions and closing the incidents. Typical incident report cycle involves

Reported -> Opened ->Assigned -> Fixed -> Closed. However the incident could be Rejected, Deferred or Reopened in few cases.

3.1.6 Tools support for testing

The benefits of using Test tools involves reduction of repetitive work. It means consistency, repeatability, objective assessment.

Classification on the basis of support for testing and tests	Test Management Tools
	Requirement Management Tools
	Incident Management Tools
	Configuration Management Tools
Static testing Tools	Review Tools
	Statuc analysis Tools
	Modeling Tools
Test specification Tools	Test design Tools
	Test data preparation Tools
Test execution and Logging	Test execution Tools
	Test harness/unit test frame works
	Test comparators
	Coverage measurement Tools
	Security testing Tools
Tools support for performance and monitoring	Dynamic analysis Tools
	Performance testing, load and stress testing Tools
	Monitoring Tools

Test Tool Classification

3.2 Certified Test Analyst

This certification tests over and above what is tested in foundation level. The course syllabus by certifying authority for example below gives the idea of what is expected.

ISTQB Test Analysts Syllabus

Chapter 1: The Technical Test Analyst's Tasks in Risk-Based Testing
- Risk identification
- Risk assessment
- Risk mitigation

Chapter 2: White-Box Test Techniques
- White-Box test techniques
- Selecting a white-box test technique

Chapter 3: Analytical Techniques
- Static analysis
- Dynamic analysis

Chapter 4: Quality Characteristics for Technical Testing
- General planning issues
- Security testing
- Reliability testing
- Performance efficiency testing
- Maintainability testing
- Portability testing
- Compatibility testing

Chapter 5: Reviews
- Using checklists in reviews
- Architectural reviews
- Code Reviews

Chapter 6: Test Tools & Automation
- Defining the test automation project
- Specific test tools

ISTQB Test Analysts Syllabus

3.3 Certified Test Manager

This certification is for test managers.

REFERENCES

1. Bath, Graham, and Erik van Veenendaal. *Improving the Test Process: Implementing Improvement and Change—a Study Guide for the ISTQB Expert Level Module*. 1st edition, Rocky Nook Inc, 2014.
2. Berk, Joseph, and Susan Berk. *Quality Management for the Technology Sector*. Newnes, 2000.
3. Black, Rex, et al. *Agile Testing Foundations: An ISTQB Foundation Level Agile Tester Guide*. 2017.
4. Black, Rex, and Jamie L. Mitchell. *Advanced Software Testing*. 1st ed, Rocky Nook, 2009.
5. Dick, Scott, and Abraham Kandel. *Computational Intelligence in Software Quality Assurance*. World Scientific, 2005.
6. *FOUNDATIONS OF SOFTWARE TESTING ISTQB CERTIFICATION, 4TH EDITION*. CENGAGE LEARNING EMEA, 2019.
7. Naik, Kshirasagar, and Priyadarshi Tripathy. *Software Testing and Quality Assurance: Theory and Practice*. John Wiley & Sons, 2008.
8. Roman, Adam. *The ISTQB Foundation Level 2018 Syllabus: Test Techniques and Sample Exams*. 1st edition, Springer Berlin Heidelberg, 2018.
9. Tian, Jeff. *Software Quality Engineering: Testing, Quality Assurance, and Quantifiable Improvement*. John Wiley & Sons, Inc., 2005. *DOI.org (Crossref)*, doi:10.1002/0471722324.

15

Software Configuration Management

S oftware configuration management is maintaining the artifacts Ex: Code, Design document, schedule, test cases , test environment scripts to name a few in version object base. Typical example tools which aid configuration management can be:

1. Clearcase
2. GitHub
3. Mercurial
4. AWS Code Commit
5. GitLAB

Further the organization may maintain the artifacts in public, private or hybrid cloud depending upon criticality of the software.

SCM Repository: The place where artifacts are stored

SCM Process: Process employed by the configuration manager (Team member) to ensure the adherence to organization process.

Summary: This chapter is about Software Configuration Management.

16

Product Metrics

According to Ejiogu the following should be true about software metrics:

1. Simple and computable: It should be easy to learn how to derive the metrics

2. Empirically and intuitively persuasive: The metric should satisfy engineers intuitive notions

3. Consistent and objective: The metrics should always yield results that are unambiguous.

4. Consistent in use of units and dimensions: Units combination should not be counter intuitive.

5. Programming language independent: Metrics should be based on requirements model, design model etc.

6. An effective mechanism for high quality feed-back: Metrics should should provide with information that can lead to higher quality end product.

Roche suggests a measurement process that can be characterized by five activities:

1. Formulation: Derivation of software metrics appropriate for the software

being considered

2. Collection: The very mechanism that is used for accumulating the data
3. Analysis: Application of Mathematical Tools
4. Interpretation: Insight into the quality of the representation
5. Feedback: Recommendations derived from the interpretation of product interpretation

There are metrics for:

1. Metrics for requirements model
2. Metrics for design model
3. Metrics for source code
4. Metrics for testing
5. Metrics for maintenance

For example metrics for object oriented design could be:

1. Size: Example count of OO entities such as classes and operation. Depth count in inheritance tree etc
2. Complexity: Example: How Classes are interrelated
3. Coupling: Example: Number of collaboration between OO entities
4. Sufficiency: Design component or Class is sufficient if it fully reflects all the properties of application domain.
5. Completeness: Example "What properties are required to fully represent the problem domain"

For example maintenance metrics could be:

Software Maturity Index = {Total modules in current release - (Modules changed/added/deleted)}/(Total modules in current release).

Summary: We discussed various aspects of product metrics in general which are also applicable to communication network software.

17

Project Management

To study the project management you NEED not have held the title "Project Manager". It is a general concept which can be learned through observation also.

As Roger S. Pressman's Book says "Effective project management focuses on four P's: people, product, process and project. The order is not arbitrary".

1. The people: Most important. Involves cultivation of motivated, highly skilled software people
2. The product: Established product objectives and scope before the project is planned
3. The process: The process provides comprehensive framework from which comprehensive plan for software development can be established
4. The project: To manage the complexity planned and controlled software projects are necessary

The WWWWWHH Principle

1. Why the system is being developed?
2. What will be done?
3. When it will be done?

4. Who is responsible for a function?
5. Where are they located organizationally?
6. How will the job be done technically and managerially?
7. How much of each resources is needed?

Summary: **In this chapter we discussed Project Management from very high level. All of it is applicable to communication network software project management.**

18

Process and Project Metrics

Measurement enables us to gain insight into the process and the project by providing mechanism for objective evaluation.

Let us begin with Grady's suggestion for "Software merics etiquette".

1. Use common sense and organizational sensitivity when interpreting the metrics data
2. Provide regular feed back to individual and teams who collect metrics
3. Don't use metrics to appraise individuls.
4. Work with practitioners and team to set clear goals and metrics
5. NEVER use metrics to threaten individual or teams
6. Metrics data that indicate a problem area should not be considered "negative"
7. Do not obsess with single metrics at the exclusion of other important metrics

Software Measurement

Software Measurement Metrics can be as follows:

1. Size oriented metrics
2. Function oriented metrics
3. Reconciling Lines of Code and function points metrics
4. Object oriented metrics
5. Use case oriented metrics

Metrics for software quality

1. Although there are many measures of software quality, correctness, maintainability, integrity and usability provide good indicators
2. Defect removal efficiency

Software Engineering Institute Guide Book

The guide book suggests the following.

1. Identify your business goals.
2. Identify what you want to learn and know
3. Identify your subgoals
4. Identify entities and attributes related to your sub goal.
5. Formalize your measurement goals
6. Identify quantifiable questions and related indicators that you will use to help you achieve measurement goals
7. Identify the data elements that you will collect to construct the indicators that help answer your questions
8. Define the measures to be used and make these definitions operational
9. Identify the actions that you will take to implement the measures
10. Prepare a plan for implementing the measures

Summary: In this chapter we discussed about process and project metrics for software in general which are also applicable to communication network software.

19

Estimation for Software Projects

E stimation is estimating the resources required and time that will elapse from start to finish.

Estimation involves decomposition techniques

1. Software sizing
2. problem based estimation
3. Lines Of Code based estimation
4. Function Point based estimation
5. Process based estimation
6. Estimation based on Use cases
7. Reconciling estimates

Few empirical estimation models

1. COCOMO II Model which stands for Constructive Cost Model
2. Structure of estimation model which can be Lines of Code oriented or Function Point oriented.
3. Software equation

Summary: We discussed about software estimation in this chapter. The empirical estimation models as it is may not suit your communication

network software project. Software Engineering Process Group of the organization should be consulted for tailor made techniques of estimation.

20

Project Scheduling

The delayed software delivery can be traced to the following root causes:

1. An unrealistic dead line established by some one outside the software team.
2. An honest underestimate of the effort and/or resources required
3. Predictable and or unpredictable risks that were not considered at the commencement of project
4. Technical difficulties that could have been foreseen in advance
5. Miscommunication
6. A failure of project management to recognize that project is falling behind the schedule and lack of action to correct it.

Basic Principles of Project Scheduling:

1. Compartmentalization
2. Interdependency
3. Time allocation
4. Effort validation
5. Defined responsibilities
6. Defined outcomes

7. Defined milestones

Some time additional people need to be added to project where tasks can be parallel to accommodate the schedule. Further effort must be distributed appropriately

Scheduling:

Following two figures show the time line chart that I had prepared for non communication software project. But the same principles should hold good for scaled (Resources+time line) communication project.

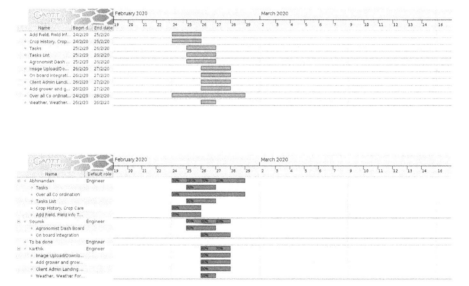

Scheduling also involves tracking the schedule it self and tracking the progress.

Summary: In this chapter we studied project scheduling and looked at over simplified time line charts for demonstration purpose.

21

Risk Management

According to Charette
" First, risk concerns future happenings. Today and yesterday are beyond active concerns, as we are already reaping what was sowed by our previous actions...............".

According to Charette

1. Risk is future happening
2. Risk involves change
3. Risk involves choice

Following points are important

1. Reactive versus proactive risk strategies: Risk management should be proactive
2. Software Risks involves uncertainty. May or may not happen. Examples include project, technical and business risks.
3. Risk identification are essentially threats to the project plan
4. Risk projection also called risk estimation tries to rate the risk on the basis of (a) Probability that risk is real (b) Consequences
5. Risk Refinement with time passage in the project.
6. Risk mitigation, monitoring and management or RMMM plan is used by

the project manager as part of over all project plan.

Summary: We studied about Risk management in software projects.

22

Maintenance and Reengineering

S oftware maintenance and re-engineering are very crucial for software product in general. Communication network software included.

Software Maintenance

Software maintenance begins almost immediately after deployment. Bug reports filter back to software engineering organization. Enhancement requests come in. This is software maintenance phase.

Software Supportability

In order to effectively support industry grade software organization must be capable of making corrections, adaptations and enhancements as requested

Software Reengineering

Involves the following activities

1. Inventory analysis
2. Document restructuring

3. Reverse engineering
4. Code restructuring
5. Data restructuring
6. Forward engineering

Reverse Engineering

Example : Extracting design information from code

Restructuring

Involves code and data restructuring

Forward Engineering

Creation of modern equivalent of older program

Summary: We discussed about maintenance and re engineering for software in general.

23

Software Process Improvements

S oftware Process Improvements (SPI) implies many things.

1. Elements of software process can be defined in an effective manner
2. Existing software development approach of the organization can be assessed
3. Meaningful strategy for improvements can be defined

Maturity Models:

- **Level 5 Optimized**
- **Level 4 Managed**
- **Level 3 Defined**
- **Level 2 Repeatable**
- **Level 1 Initial**

Summary: We discussed about Software Process Improvements

24

Emerging Communication Software

1. **Internet of Things**
2. 5 G
3. **Satellite communication**

Parting Notes

An attempt is made to describe software engineering for communication network software in less than 100 pages, a subject which is easily worth at-least 1000 pages.